60 WAYS TO PROPOSE

and Other Important Secrets

[second edition]

Monica Cyr

Cold Rock Publishing is a TradeMark
of La Vella Entertainment Group Inc

60 Ways to Propose and Other Important Secrets

Second Edition 2012
ESBN 978-0973552621

Web: coldrockpublishing.com
Web: lavellagroup.com

This book and all my works are
dedicated to my inspiration,
my motivation,
my best friend,
and true love, my husband,
Louie.

CONTENTS

INTRODUCTION

Talking to both my girl and guy friends, it seems that's many men have no idea what a girl expects for a proposal. Most females go through their whole lives dreaming about this special moment. This places all the pressure on men to fulfil those dreams.

That is why I wanted to create this book. I would hate for any man to feel like he can't fulfil his partner's dream of having a romantic, adventurous, or special proposal. I would also hate for any woman to think that their man hasn't put a lot of thought into the proposal.

This book is split up into a variety of categories to make it easier to find the proposal that is right for you. Starting off with special occasions, this section refers to creative proposals for every type of holiday.

Depending on the type of person your partner is, you may be looking for a romantic proposal, an adventurous proposal, or a proposal everyone will see.

I placed a section, *At Their Work*, in this book for those who would like to surprise their partner at work. Take this section with caution. I recommend that you receive permission first from your partner's boss or company before surprising them with a proposal. This may also help you plan out your proposal since you may need their assistance. For each proposal I have listed the type of work first, as well as the assistance you may need from co-workers.

Lastly, I have included the least expensive to no-cost-at-all proposals for those who may be on a tight budget. However, these ideas are great for anyone. They could also be included under Romantic or Creative, so don't skip this section simply because you feel like spending lots of money for a proposal. You may also find these proposals under other headings as well.

Good luck to all of you who are planning the proposal. I hope you find this book extremely helpful and I wish you all the best in your future marriage.

This is a new chapter to the rest of your life! Congratulations!

PART ONE

The Proposal

SPECIAL OCCASIONS

On her birthday, make up a bunch of clues that lead to different places around the house. Take the first clue and stick it outside the door so your partner finds it when they get home. This clue will then lead to another clue somewhere in the house. For something extra, you can also add a present with each clue. If you really want to be creative, have the present be something related to weddings, such as a magazine. Then have a series of clues until the last one, which leads her to where you are (preferably where she won't be looking for a clue so she doesn't find you before finishing the hunt!). Once she find you, she gets the last present – a ring!

For Christmas, get her something that is not what she expected. An example of this could be something to clean the house with (I take this example from my father who gave my mom a Swiffer for Christmas one year and has never lived it down!). Give it to her for Christmas, making her think this is her present. After her disappointment is apparent and she has opened all her other gifts, give her the ring and your proposal as her final present.

This proposal will work only for those who do not have a pet and want one! For any special occasion where gifts are exchanged, buy her a pet. A dog or a cat would be perfect for a proposal. The day you want to give it to her, tie a ribbon around it's neck. Around the ribbon, tie the ring you will use for the proposal. Then give her the animal and wait until she notices the ring. Once she notices, officially ask for her hand in marriage.

For her birthday, a cake is mandatory. But instead of buying her one, make one yourself. This works even better if you can't make cakes because it will show that you tried really hard! On the top of the cake, write 'will you marry me' on it and have a thick candle with a ring on it sitting next to the phrase.

This idea can be used for any occasion where gifts are given. Collect a variety of boxes, making sure to have one huge box and all the others being able to fit into one another. Take the ring box, wrap it up, then put it into a box a little bigger than the ring box. Then wrap up that box and place it in a box a little bigger than that one. Continue like this until you have one very large box that is wrapped up. You may want to add some rocks to each of the boxes just to make the present heavy. Give the large wrapped box to your partner for her birthday, Christmas, or Valentine's Day. She will have no idea that in this large box lies a ring. Watch as she unwraps the first box, the second, third, and so on. As she gets closer to the ring box, you know that's what she is hoping for, so get on your knee, take her hand, and get ready to propose when she gets to the last box.

For Christmas or New Year's Eve, make her a calendar. This calendar will be titled 'will you marry me?' and the entire year will have dates of bridal shows, appointments with possible reception halls, and your possible wedding dates! This calendar might take a bit of planning, so start making it with plenty of time before your proposal. It also will take some research to find out the dates of bridal shows, call ahead to book appointments with reception sites, and plan anything else you might add to the surprise. It might be good to get some help from your partner's best girlfriend, since she might know more about all the bridal stuff than you will. When the time comes, present your partner with the calendar and a ring.

On New Year's Eve, go to a big city (New York City would be the biggest!) for the festivities. Find a cameraman for the local news station and ask him if you can propose to your partner live on television right before the New Year. When the time is right, bring your partner over to the camera and talk about New Year's with the host. Pull out the ring and propose to your partner, live in front of thousands!

At Christmas parties or other occasions, you may find a magician performs. If you are aware of anyone who may be having a magician for an occasion, ask the name and number of the magician. Give him or her a call and let them know that you would like them to help you plan out your proposal. Work it so that during one of their tricks, the magician makes a ring box appear (the one you give him or her beforehand). Then have him/her ask for a volunteer, and of course have them pick you. With you on stage, have the magician ask you to open the box and tell the audience how you feel. This is your cue to open the box, get on your knee and give your wife-to-be your proposal.

ROMANTIC

Fill her bedroom with roses before she gets home. On each rose, put a tag that says something that you love about her (each one must be different, of course). Make a trail of petals to her room. Right before she gets home, go to her room and stand in the middle with a rose and a tag, with the ring, that asks her to marry you.

On a nice day, take your partner to a romantic picnic at a local park or a secluded area. Towards the end of the perfect meal, pull out the ring and ask her to have you for life.

Take your partner to her favourite restaurant. With pervious planning, ask the manager to have the following as a menu choice:

WILL YOU MARRY ME
Filled with a lifetime of loving and caring, this choice includes a promise of breakfast in bed, care of you while sick, and a life with adventure and romance.

When you get to the restaurant, be sure the waiter is aware of the previously created menu and give it to your partner. Allow her time to find it for herself, and when she does, pull out the ring to show her you are serious.

Make a dinner with the menu full of ring-type foods. You can make onion rings, donuts, chicken breasts with a hole cut in the middle, and potato slices baked with a hole cut in the middle. Add some circular, wreath-type candles for the table. Then after the meal, present the last 'ring' with your proposal.

If you have a long distance relationship and will not see your partner for while, this is a great way to propose before you see her. Find a picture of a ring and cut it out into a few pieces (enough so you can put it back together again). Each day, send a piece to your partner. With the last piece, send a card proclaiming your love for her as well as your proposal. Once you see her, complete the proposal with a real ring.

Take your partner on a vacation to a place with a beach. Be sure to request a hotel room that faces the beach. Before your partner wakes up, sneak out to the beach and write 'will you marry me' into the sand so it can be seen from your room. If it is wet outside, you might want to write out the words with rocks instead. Then go back and wake up your partner. Take her to the window or balcony to show her what you've done, then get one your knee with the ring.

If you have talents in music, write her a song about how much she means to you. Include your proposal at the end. Take her to a special spot, or anywhere you are both comfortable, and sing it to her, presenting a ring at the end.

Go to a shop that lets you make your own wine. With one of the bottles you make, print off a label that has a poem you have written about her along with the proposal. During a romantic dinner, give the bottle to your partner for her to read. Be prepared to pull out the ring when she finishes reading.

Before your partner gets home, sprinkle fresh rose petals along the floor leading up to the bedroom (or any room you choose). Have the room be full of flowers and candles, and you in the middles with the ring. When your partner gets home, they will follow the trail of petals straight to your proposal.

Buy a variety of flowers, which makes up close to one hundred individual flowers. Early one morning, before your partner has woken up, set up on the lawn or driveway in front of her bedroom window. Place the flowers in a pattern that spells our 'marry me'. Be sure that it is big enough for her to read when she wakes up. With any extra flowers, wrap them up and prepare to give them to her when she awakens. Once you have finished your project, ring her doorbell. When she comes to the door, give her the flowers and tell her to go back to her room and look outside the window. Follow her up there and as she looks out the window, get on your knee and pull out the ring. When she turns around you can ask her again to marry you (she will still want to hear it from your mouth).

ADVENTUROUS AND PUBLIC

For the more adventurous type, a bungee jump can be a great way to propose. Go with your mate to an amusement park that has a place to bungee jump. Tell her to wait at the bottom for you and to videotape your jump. Once you get to the top, wave to your partner, and make sure she's taping you. Then right before you jump, say "*her name*, I need to ask you a question" and then take the jump while screaming "marry me?" When you get to the bottom, ask her again, this time with the ring. The great thing is that she will have it all on tape for you both to watch over and over again.

This proposal is perfect for the outdoor and adventurous type of people. Plan to take your partner for a weekend of hiking through the mountains or hills. Depending on where you are living, you might have to turn this into a small vacation to a mountain range. Pick your proposal spot ahead of time, which should be at the top of the mountain, or hill, or the spot you plan on stopping to eat. Visit this spot the day before or of your hike (preferably early morning when your partner is not awake, otherwise sneak out for a bit) and place a flag there that says "you made it to this milestone, lets take it to the next". Before you actually go for the hike, make sure not to forget the ring! Then hike with your partner to the spot you had chosen. Let her read the flag while you get out the ring. After she reads the flag, ask her to take the next step by marrying you.

Call an amusement park that has a roller coaster that goes through a tunnel (which many parks do). Arrange something with them so that you can have a glow-in-the-dark sign placed in the tunnel that asks your partner to marry you. Decide with the park which day you will be taking your partner there so the sign may be displayed. Take your partner on the appropriate day. Try to get to the tunnel ride first to avoid wait times (waiting will only make you nervous). Hint to your partner that you heard something about that ride having signs in the tunnel. This way she will be looking for signs during the ride. After she sees the sign, complete the moment with an official proposal from you. When the ride stops, give her the ring.

At almost any sports event (baseball, hockey, football, etc.) is a stadium with a jumbo screen. For a fee of usually under $100, you can request birthday's and anniversary's to be announced on the screen by talking to someone from the customer service office. In this case, ask them to post your proposal up on the screen during the game. When the time comes, point your partner to the way of the screen and celebrate the excitement with thousands of other people!

If your city or town has billboards available for rental, find out from city hall how much it would cost to rent one. Have a simple proposal printed on it. Take your mate on a walk or drive past it and when she notices that the proposal is for her, pull out the ring to make it complete.

On nice days, small planes are often sent by companies to fly around with a banner attached to them with an ad or message on it. This usually is popular on beaches that are populated with thousands of people. If you live in this type of area rent one of those banners with 'will you marry me _her name_' on it. Then take her for a day at the beach where the banner will be flying for her - and all - to see.

Talk to a local comedy club or theatre and arrange for an opportunity for you to get up on stage and propose to your partner during one of their shows. Then book tickets and take her to the performance. In the middle of the show, tell her you have to go to the bathroom and sneak backstage. When the time comes, go out on stage and surprise her with your proposal in front of the entire audience.

At your favourite movie theatre, ask the manager if you can borrow space on the sign that lists all the movies that are playing. On this space, have your proposal put up. Take your mate to the movie theatre and let her read out the movie choices. When she gets to your proposal, slip the ring on her finger!

At air shows, some pilots can write messages in the sky with white smoke. If you know of air shows in your area, know a friend who is a pilot, or you are a pilot yourself, this idea will be perfect! During an air show, have one of the planes spell out "MARRY ME" with the plane. Turn to your partner, get on your knee, and give her the ring.

Depending on how risky you want to be, go to a tattoo parlour and have the proposal written somewhere on your body. If you are a little less into the risk-taking, get henna or a fake tattoo placed on your body that includes your proposal.

At most movie theatres, there is a slide show of ads for people to see while they are waiting for their movie to start. Talk to the manager of one of these theatres and ask to rent an ad for one night. Design the ad however you like for a proposal. Then take her to see that movie the night you rented out the ad. Be sure to get there early so you don't miss your proposal being shown!

If you have a friend who is a police officer, or if you are an officer yourself, this is a great way to propose! Talk to an officer who is unknown to your partner. Arrange with him or her a day, time, and place that you would like him/her to pull you over. With your partner in the car, have the police officer waiting in a pre-determined spot. When you pass by, have the officer pull you over and ask you to step out of the car because you are under arrest. When your partner sees this, she won't understand what is going on. Have the officer ask her to step outside the car and come beside you. Then the officer will read you your rights, which has to include "the right to ask *her name* to marry you". Then get on your knee and propose to your confused partner!

Take your partner to a karaoke bar with all your friends one night. Ask the DJ to give you a song to sing that involves the idea of marriage, love, or request to sing one of her favourite songs. When it is your turn to sing, be sure you have a ring ready. Sing her the song and when you are finished, ask her to marry you in front of everyone!

Find out when her favourite band is in town and buy tickets for you both. Get in contact with the concert promotor or tour manager of the group themselves. Try to find someone you can talk to about the band announcing the engagement for you while they are on stage. When the spotlight is on you and your partner is confused, get on your knee and propose to her.

If your partner loves art, look for an art show that is coming up in your area. Talk to the place that is holding the show and ask if you can place a painting there that has your proposal on it. Then, on the day of the show, take your partner to see the special piece of art. Once she comes upon the proposal painting, get on your knee and slip the ring on her finger!

Visit your local newspaper and ask them if you can place an ad in the paper. Design an ad that has the story of how you met, and how your partner has changed your life, and so on. The in large letters on the ad, have your proposal written. The entire community will have a chance to read your story and proposal along with your future bride!

CREATIVE

Design a scrapbook with everything from your earliest memories together, to movie ticket stubs, to napkins from favourite restaurants, to vacation pictures. On the last page of the scrapbook, make a proposal. For example, you could design it with wedding-type pictures and write a letter or a poem on it with your proposal at the end. While your partner is reading it, get on your knee and be prepared to pull out that ring!

A video proposal is definitely a creative idea. There is a variety of ways you can go about doing this. You act out the story of how you met using dolls, puppets, or yourself, and tape it. You can just sit in front of the camera and tell her how you feel. You can pretend to be doing a news story and interview friends and family about the relationship or about your partner. There are many ways to do this, these are just a few. But a video of your proposal is great for people who may be too nervous to propose in person or for someone who wants to say the right thing and not want to forget to say anything. Using a video, you can do it over and over until you get it right!

Many large craft stores have books, or even seminars, that teach you how to make a candle. When making a candle, you can stick things in (like charms or coins) that will only appear once the candle has melted. Make a candle with the ring inside, so it cannot be seen until the candle has melted. Give her the candle as a present and tell her there is another present inside the candle. Have a romantic dinner as you watch the candle burn. Once the ring has appeared, blow the candle out and wait for the ring to cool down. Then have her pull it out and propose!

Collect as many pictures as you can of your mate when she was younger. Talk to her family about this one so she has no idea you are up to something. Get pictures from the time she was born to the time that you both met. Do the same for yourself. Once you have collected everything, create a slideshow. Set up the pictures by having one picture being of her, the next of you, then of her, and then you, and so on. Start with baby pictures and move all the way through both of your lives until you reach pictures of the both of you together. Have the very last slide be your proposal. Then whisk her away on a night of laughter and memories as you think back to all the events in the pictures. Of course, be ready with the ring for the last slide.

If you are talented in drama or theatre, put on a little play for her one day. This can be done on your own or with the use of puppets. Write the script to fit the way you met and how much better she has made your life. You can exaggerate things to make them more humorous. Then plan a day to put on the play for her and act out the script. At the end of the play, be sure to recite a poem or letter that includes your proposal, then get on your knee and place the ring on her finger.

Websites are simple to build, as there as there are many free templates available for those without any technical knowledge at all. Create a webpage for your proposal. Design it with pictures of the two of you from vacations, holidays, and anything else you may have. Add a poem about love or write one yourself about her. Have your proposal written somewhere on the page. When the time is right, ask her to go to that site and be prepared to pull out the ring.

If she enjoys puzzles, create one for her! Use bristol board to design a puzzle. You can draw things, use pictures of you both, or cut out pictures from magazines. Add 'will you marry me' to it. Once your masterpiece is completed, cut it up into a few pieces and give it to your partner to complete. After she figures out the message, slip the ring on her finger!

Create a word search for your partner. Use words that involve romance or weddings. Try to fill up as much space as you can. Then with the spaces that are left over, use the letters 'w-i-l-l-u-m-a-r-r-y-m-e' to fill in the spots. Ask her to unscramble the letters to make a phrase. Once she figures out what you are asking, offer her the ring.

AT THEIR WORK

Teacher
With previous permission from the principal, during the morning or afternoon announcements on the PA system announce that you would like to know if Ms. _her name_ would marry you. Then show up to her classroom with the ring in hand.

Teacher
When the school has an assembly, assign some of the kids in the school (with help from the principal) to bring your partner a flower. After ten or more students have given her a flower, come into the assembly. In front of everyone in the school, propose to her!

Drive-Thru Person
During a slow time, go up to the drive-thru and ask if you can order a yes from them to go with your question of 'do you want to marry me?'

Dentist/Dental Assistant
There are special places where you can get jewels or writing on your teeth that last for up to a month. Get writing on

your teeth that says 'marry me' (but using something that will come off in less than a month!). Then book and appointment with your partner, but under a different name so they don't know it will be you. When you go for your appointment, just smile at her and she will get the message!

Workplace with message board
Places such as restaurants, car dealerships, cinemas, etc., have message boards on their property. Have the words "will you marry me *her name*?' placed on the message board early one morning. Be there before she arrives and stand under or beside the sign, with ring in hand.

Working at a computer
Sneak into your partner's work before she gets there and change her screen saver or desktop to say "WILL YOU MARRY ME". Then hide somewhere in the office to jump out with a ring for when she reads it.

Student
Speak with your partner's professor and ask him or her to announce the proposal in the middle of class. Once it is

announced, come into the room with flowers and a ring in hand.

Doctor/Nurse in a hospital
After planning with her co-workers, page your partner with the emergency code, sending her to the operating room or whatever room you choose to give her. The room that she will be sent to should first be decorated with candles and flowers. Once you have paged her, go to the room yourself and be ready on one knee and with the ring for when she comes running in. Once she gets there, give her your proposal!

LEAST EXPENSIVE

Call a local radio station and request a song that means something to the both of you. Ask the announcer to say the proposal before he or she plays the song, or ask the announcer if they will put you on the air to propose yourself. The only catch is that you need to have your partner listening at that specific time! But even if they miss it, you can still record the proposal and play it back for them later.

Call your local newspaper and ask them if they can do a story on your partner. Some small community papers look for stories where people are given recognition for work that they do in the community. Instead, ask the editors if they will write about your partner in terms of how they changed your life and about your relationship. Have a proposal at the end of the article. Some newspapers will do this, especially if they are small and looking for content. Your best time to do this would be around Valentine's Day, since stories on love and relationships are popular around this time.

Bake your partner's favourite cookies and put the ring inside of one of them. Be sure part of the ring is sticking out just in case they try to swallow the cookie whole! Then make them eat the cookies until the one with the ring is found.

After taking a hot shower (so the mirror is foggy), write the words 'will you marry me' on the mirror with your finger. Let your mate take a shower next and when she gets out to see the message, be on your knees with the ring, and proposal on the mirror.

If you have a close-knit family, a family picnic is a great place to propose. With everyone there while eating, give a toast to the family and give a speech about how you would love for your partner to join the family, and propose. This saves you a lot of phone calls, since everyone important was there to share in the excitement! To make the memory last forever, tell one of the relatives about your plan to propose and ask them to record the moment.

Before she gets back from work, place love notes all around the house and find a hiding spot for yourself. Have the first note telling her to collect all the notes. Once she's seemed to have found all the notes, come out of your hiding spot with the ring and propose.

If your partner is a party girl and loves to drink beer, this proposal will work for you. Many beer companies like to give away prizes in their cases of beer, usually a shirt. For her birthday, buy her one of these cases of beer and pull out the prize. Replace the prize with a shirt you make yourself that says 'will you marry me' (use fabric paint or markers on a plain t-shirt). You can also tie the ring to one of the bottles or cans if you like. Then wrap up the case and have her open it on her birthday. It will be the best present she ever had!

Carnivals occur almost every weekend at some mall, or larger carnivals each year in every city. The day you want to propose, talk to a guy that runs one of the carnival games. Tell him you will be coming back with your partner and will be coming to play that game. Give him a bear that you want to win that has a shirt on it saying 'marry me' (if you trust the guy, tie the ring around the bear's neck, otherwise tie a cheap ring around it's neck and present the real ring when you win the prize). Then bring your partner back and have her play the game. Whether she wins or not, the carnival guy will give her the bear. While she reads its shirt, get on your knee and take the ring from the bear's neck and place it on her finger.

Memory lane is always a great place to propose. Take your mate back to the place where you first met. Even act out the way you met, if you choose to do so. Remember each moment and how you both felt about each other that day. Then when the time is right, ask her to continue those memories forever and marry you.

PART TWO

The Secrets

PROPOSAL ETIQUETTE

The etiquette for proposing is not set in stone. Traditionally, men propose to women, but today's society allows for the exception to this rule. More than ever, women are proposing to men.

The men, however, do not always appreciate this. The thrill of the chase comes naturally to men. Therefore many feel that it is their duty to propose as their way of 'catching' the woman. Most men said they would much rather propose than be proposed to because that's they way it is supposed to be. It's tough to break tradition.

Another concern in proposing is the question of the in-laws. Again, tradition calls for asking your mate's parents for her hand in marriage before asking your mate. This tradition is not as apparent as it once was. But, depending on your mate, her parents might expect this. Some cultures firmly believe in the parental blessings before the engagement. So it is important to know what her culture's traditions are.

This also is true of some family's values. Those that are set in older traditions may expect their future son to ask them for permission to marry their daughter. If you know her family (which you should if you plan on marrying her!), then you will know whether or not they expect you to ask permission. Even if they don't expect that, it is still respectful to do so.

The last part on etiquette is getting on your knee when you propose.

CHOOSING RINGS

The ring is an important part of the engagement because it signifies the commitment you are forming with your partner. However, the media plays a major role in making buyers believe that the bigger the diamond, the more you love her. This is obviously not the case, but some women expect that. You will know whether your partner expects a large rock based on her personality. For instance, if she likes material things, she will probably expect a bigger ring. Still, there are many men who have no idea what their women want. The following paragraphs will give you some ideas what to do based on your situation.

This first situation is for men who want to propose without their partner knowing, but who also do not know what their mate wants in terms of a ring. In this case, you may have to give her two rings. First, buy a less expensive ring to actually propose with. This way she will have no idea that you were planning to propose. After the engagement, take her to a jewellery store and buy her the ring she wants. If she ends up wanting to keep the one you gave her, that's a bonus!

The next situation is for men who want to propose with the right ring, but do not know what their mate wants. In this case, take her shopping and casually bring her into a jewellery store, asking her what she likes. You don't have to tell her that you are planning a proposal, but she will probably suspect it. However, you are still keeping mysterious by not asking her exactly what she wants you to buy her for an engagement ring. Take note of what she looks at and come back later to pick a ring from the ones she pointed out to you.

The last situation is the case of men who want to propose with the exact ring their partner wants and do not care if they know about the proposal. In this case, take her to the jewellery store and get her to pick one out. You can also tell her that she can get it at anytime, soon or later. This way she will be anxiously waiting, but will still not know when she will be proposed to.

TIPS ON YOUR PROPOSAL

Being female, there are a variety of tips I have for you to complete the perfect proposal. Through first hand experience as well as expectations from friends, I have an idea about what most woman are looking for in a proposal. This section will let you in on everything from what females expect to what would pleasantly surprise them.

The first and best tip I can give you is to choose a proposal that suits her. Again, you know your partner best. Therefore you will know whether she would want something private and low key or something adventurous and public. Pick something that suits her personality. The examples in this book can fit a vast amount of personalities, from the romantics to the party animals. Just be sure not to pick something that doesn't fit your partner's desires.

Try to record your proposal. Any woman would love to look back on that moment and relive it over and over again. This can be done in a variety of ways. For those that decide to propose publicly, anyone in public can easily tape you. For instance, if you are going to propose in a restaurant, get someone you know to be there at the same time to video the proposal. However, you must be certain that anyone recording the moment isn't seen by your partner. Just make sure they are to your partner's back. Once you propose, the person recording can come right up to the both of you. Neither of you will probably even notice, since you will be too caught up in the moment.

Remember to stay in your budget. If you cannot afford an expensive proposal, don't plan on one! The simple and heart-felt proposals are often the ones that are the best. Stay within your financial capabilities. Besides, you will have to start saving for the wedding.

If you are proposing in a non-public place, have a camera set up where your partner won't notice, but that will catch the proposal. A word of caution, however, if you know your partner does not like to be on video, then do not video the proposal. You know your partner best and if you think that she will be upset with a video of her, then don't do it. Use your discretion.

Also, put thought into the proposal. Just purchasing this book proves that you have taken this step. However, go a little further by actually planning and organizing what it is that you want to do. Each one of the ideas in this book involves planning. Therefore, you have pretty much covered this tip if you choose and idea from here.

I should also suggest that you try to make something yourself. Home made cards, poems, or letters impress many females. This isn't something that must be done, but it would certainly be a pleasant surprise for the wife-to-be if you wrote her a poem. Again, it depends on the female as to whether or not this would touch her heart. So again, it's your call!

A tip for your own sanity would be to give your proposal as early in the day as you can. Men tend to be nervous about proposing, and it will show. Your partner will notice you acting differently as you get more anxious the day you plan to propose. Therefore, proposing earlier in the day will prevent all the anxiety you might feel, and your partner will be less likely to notice your excitement. This might not work for everyone, but if your proposal time is flexible, it's better that you do it in the morning for your own sake!

Furthering the idea of keeping yourself calm, do not use alcohol to do so! If you are nervous about the proposal and start drinking, you may find that it keeps you calm. But if you get drunk, you are in no condition to be proposing to you mate. So, as much as alcohol might help you calm down, try not to drink unless it is champagne to toast your future wife!

The last and very important tip is to enjoy the moment! Try not to focus entirely on the proposal, but what the proposal signifies.

HOW NOT TO PROPOSE

As well as ways *to* propose, it is just as important to hear about ways *not to* propose. The following is a real-life story of a proposal that should not have been! Needless to say, this couple is still together!

"Richard and I and another couple were having a card game. We had all been drinking, of course, and Richard asked me if I would come to the bedroom for a minute. We went to the bedroom he sat me down, and said 'we should get married'. A couple of days later we went to the local jewellery store and he bought me a ring!"

-   Eileen and Richard
    Married 25 years

Find more great books from Cold Rock
Publishing at our website:

http://www.coldrockpublishing.com

www.ingramcontent.com/pod-product-compliance
Lightning Source LLC
Chambersburg PA
CBHW071435040426
42445CB00012BA/1364